It's Up to Us

Luisa Uribe

It's Up to Us

Building a Brighter Future for Nature, People & Planet

The Children's Terra Carta

by Christopher Lloyd

foreword by

HRH The Prince of Wales

With illustrations by

Phùng Nguyên Quang & Huỳnh Kim Liên, Peter Sís,
Stuart Armstrong, Luisa Uribe, Gunnella,
Fotini Tikkou, Raúl Colón, Murat Kalkavan,
Poonam Mistry, Estelí Meza, Mehrdokht Amini,
Sydney Smith, Vanina Starkoff, Wesley Bedrosian,
Nick Hayes, Rutu Modan, Gwen Keraval, Isol,
Nick Sharratt, Blak Douglas, Ye Luying, Sally Deng,
Owen Davey, Su Jung Jang, Paolo Domeniconi,
Victoria Fomina, Reza Dalvand, Musa Omusi,
Leah Marie Dorion, Sally Caulwell, Harmony Becker,
Barry Falls, and Kumiko Horibe.

What on Earth Books

The author would like to thank the following for their great support, encouragement, and advice in the creation of this book:
HRH The Prince of Wales, Simon Sadinsky, Jennifer Jordan-Saifi, Emily Cherrington, Jacqueline Farrell, Joanne Dempster, Richard Dunne, Chris Martin and all the team at The Prince's Foundation, and the Sustainable Markets Initiative. Also to: Keith Breslauer, Sir Robert Worcester, and all the team at What on Earth Books. And to Virginia, Matilda, and Verity Lloyd for their love and support.

Finally, I would like to dedicate this book to Satish Kumar,
the Indian British environmental campaigner and editor of *Resurgence Magazine,* who has done so much
over a lifetime to focus the world's attention, including mine, to the enormous challenges faced by Nature, People, and Planet.

—CL

What on Earth Books is an imprint of What on Earth Publishing
Allington Castle, Maidstone, Kent ME16 0NB, United Kingdom
30 Ridge Road Unit B, Greenbelt, Maryland, 20770, United States

First published in the United States in 2022

Text by Christopher Lloyd copyright © 2021 What on Earth Publishing Ltd.

Illustration on cover and pages 46–47 copyright © 2021 Phùng Nguyên Quang & Huỳnh Kim Liên;
endsheet illustration copyright © 2021 Peter Sís; spiral illustrations on i, 1, 11, 21, 33, and 56 copyright © 2021 Stuart Armstrong;
Illustration on pages ii–iii copyright © 2021 Luisa Uribe; Illustration on pages vi–vii copyright © 2021 Gunnella;
Illustration on pages viii–1 copyright © 2021 Fotini Tikkou; Illustration on pages 2–3 copyright © 2021 Raúl Colón;
Illustration on pages 4–5 copyright © 2021 Murat Kalkavan; Illustration on pages 6–7 copyright © 2021 Poonam Mistry;
Illustration on page 8 copyright © 2021 Estelí Meza; Illustration on page 9 copyright © 2021 Mehrdokht Amini;
Illustration on pages 10–11 copyright © 2021 Sydney Smith; Illustration on pages 12–13 copyright © 2021 Vanina Starkoff;
Illustration on pages 14–15 copyright © 2021 Wesley Bedrosian; Illustration on pages 16–17 copyright © 2021 Nick Hayes;
Illustration on pages 18–19 copyright © 2021 Rutu Modan; Illustration on pages 20–21 copyright © 2021 Gwen Keraval;
Illustration on pages 22–23 copyright © 2021 Isol; Illustration on pages 24–25 copyright © 2021 Nick Sharratt;
Illustration on pages 26–27 copyright © 2021 Blak Douglas; Illustration on pages 28–29 copyright © 2021 Ye Luying;
Illustration on pages 30–31 copyright © 2021 Sally Deng; Illustration on pages 32–33 copyright © 2021 Owen Davey;
Illustration on pages 34–35 copyright © 2021 Su Jung Jang; Illustration on pages 36–37 copyright © 2021 Paolo Domeniconi;
Illustration on page 38 copyright © 2021 Victoria Fomina; Illustration on page 39 copyright © 2021 Reza Dalvand;
Illustration on pages 40–41 copyright © 2021 Musa Omusi; Illustration on pages 42–43 copyright © 2013 Leah Marie Dorion;
Illustration on pages 44–45 copyright © 2021 Sally Caulwell; Illustration on pages 48–49 copyright © 2021 Harmony Becker;
Illustrations on page 54 copyright © 2021 Barry Falls; back cover illustration copyright © 2021 Kumiko Horibe.

Staff for this book: Nancy Feresten, Publisher and Editor; Bea Jackson, Art Direction and Design; Katy Lennon, Project Editor;
Andy Forshaw, Design Director; Alenka Oblak, Production Manager; Patrick Skipworth, Executive Editor.

Library of Congress Cataloging-in-Publication Data available upon request

ISBN: 978-1-9137505-6-5
OS/Toluca, Mexico/09/2021

Printed in Mexico

1 3 5 7 9 10 8 6 4 2

whatonearthbooks.com

What on Earth Books is proud to be allied with the Sustainable Markets Initiative.

Terra Carta is a Trade Mark of the Sustainable Markets Initiative.

This book was printed in Mexico on paper grown in a PEFC-certified forest.

For further information please visit www.whatonearthbooks.com/its-up-to-us

CONTENTS

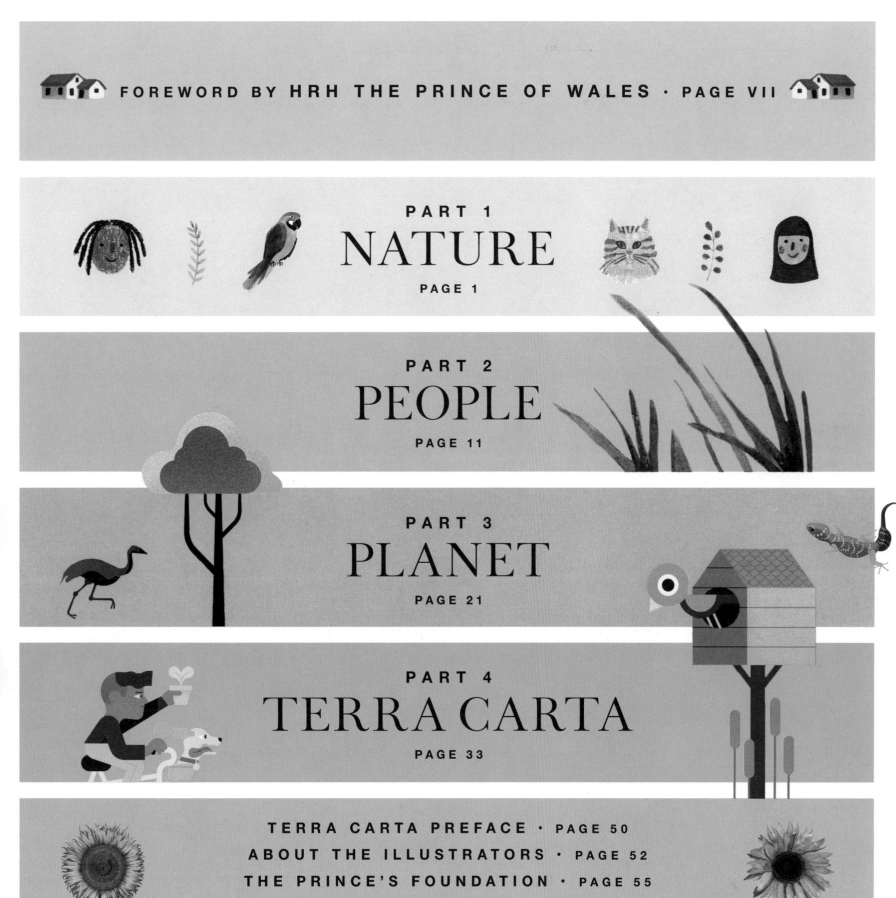

CLARENCE HOUSE

Children have a unique curiosity for Nature and for this amazing planet we call home. This is because part of being young is knowing that we are, in fact, part of Nature ourselves.

When we view a picture of the Earth from space it is easy to see how the land, water and air are one fragile system working in harmony to support life. This system contains an incredibly beautiful diversity of animals, trees, plants, flowers and insects, all of which combine to provide the ingredients for life to flourish. This web of life inspires me every day – seeing that everything is, in some way, connected to everything else.

To keep this web of life within our planet healthy, all the people in the world need to do everything they can to keep Nature healthy so that people and animals can be healthy too. This means that we need all of the world's countries, cities, businesses and organizations to work together. This is why I created the Terra Carta as a roadmap for Nature, People and Planet and is why I need your help. I hope that the story told in this book, together with the marvellous illustrations by artists from around the globe, will inspire you to discover and celebrate the natural world around you, to explore the lessons Nature has to offer and the ways that you can act to protect it.

What the world needs is for children all around it to imagine the type of future you want to build. I don't know about you, but I love to draw and paint, like many of the artists in this book. So here's my challenge to you: take out a blank piece of paper and draw, paint or write about the future you would like to see, one that puts Nature at the heart of everything we do. That way we can share our ideas with as many people as possible and, together, we can help make our planet strong and healthy for generations to come.

PART 1

NATURE

We live our lives
surrounded by people
and other living things.

Raúl Colón

Plants spring up in
parks, woods, backyards—
even in cracks in the pavements.

Animals are everywhere, too,
swimming in the ocean,
singing from the trees,
and purring in your lap.

Microbes, tiny creatures
we can only see with a microscope,
live in every nook and cranny of the Earth.
If you look closely enough,
you can find them
in the deepest parts of the sea,
the driest deserts,
inside our stomachs,
and even between our toes!

All living things nestle
in our Earth's thin outer layer,
which is made up of
three very precious things—
the air, the soil, and the oceans.

These give us the oxygen we breathe
and the wind, water, and food
that all life depends on.

The air, soil, oceans,
and all living things,
including people, form a circle
that we call Nature.
People are part of Nature,
but Nature has been around
for billions of years, from long
before humans existed.

Of the unimaginably large number
of planets in our vast universe,
Earth is the only one
that we are sure has life.
That makes our world
a truly wonderous place
and Nature
an infinitely precious thing.

PART 2

PEOPLE

Humans find everything
we need in the Nature
that surrounds us.

People have worked out
how to use other animals,
plants, rocks, air—
and even liquids and gases
found deep within the Earth—
to help us live more comfortable lives.
We use them to make
medicines and houses
and furniture and clothes
and cars and toys and gadgets
and lots and lots of other stuff.

But, because there are nearly
eight billion of us humans,
all of this happy living
has an ugly side.

The way we usually
make things and grow food
releases pollution.
This poisons the air and water
and kills the tiny living things
that keep our soil healthy.

With so many of us making, buying, selling,

and throwing away so much stuff,

mountains of garbage

and rivers of pollution

are finding their way into the oceans.

Some pollution makes the ocean more acidic,

threatening the survival of sea life,

including precious corals.

Many plants and animals are becoming extinct.

That means they are gone—

forever.

For a long time,
people thought that
because there were so many
animals and plants,
such a big wide ocean,
and lots of air and soil,
we could go on
like this forever.

Other living things

might suffer,

but not us—

"We're people," we thought,

"we'll be okay!"

We forgot that

we were Nature, too.

PART 3

PLANET

Then
we noticed something—
the Earth is getting hotter.

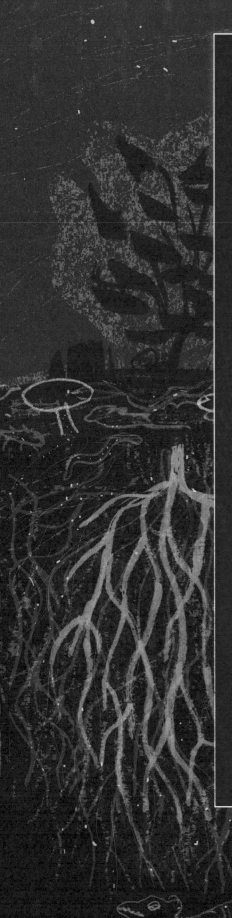

Ever since the Earth was formed
more than four billion years ago,
its temperature has been changing.

This is because a gas in the air
called carbon dioxide
captures heat from the Sun.
It works like a blanket, keeping the Earth warm.

With too little carbon dioxide in the air,
the Earth gets colder,
with glaciers stretching halfway around the world.
With too much carbon dioxide,
the Earth gets warmer, the ice melts,
and water floods onto the land.

Carbon (one of the elements in carbon dioxide)
is also found in living things.
When they die, their bodies break down,
and the carbon in them
becomes part of the soil and the oceans.

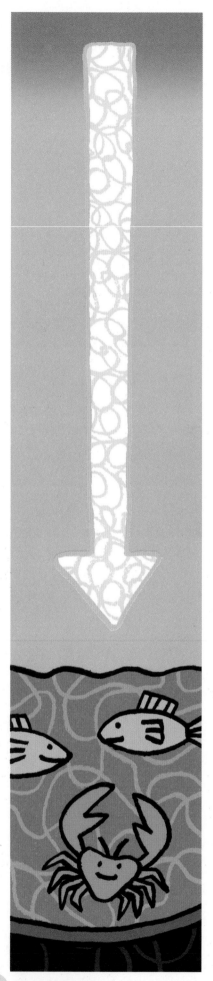

Over millions of years,
billions of tons of carbon
from dead animals and plants
gets buried deeper and
deeper under the ground and under the sea.
Eventually it turns into coal,
oil, and natural gas.
We call these substances
fossil fuels
because they were once
the remains of living things.

When we burn fossil fuels
to heat our homes,
run our cars,
and make electricity,
the carbon is released back into the air
as carbon dioxide,
making the Earth warmer and warmer.
And that is a big problem.

1 Carbon dioxide is absorbed by living things, such as trees and shellfish, and when they die, it gets trapped in the Earth.

2 Carbon from the remains of living things eventually turns into fossil fuels.

3 Fossil fuels are pumped to the Earth's surface.

4 When humans use fossil fuels, carbon dioxide is released into the air.

Too much carbon dioxide
is making storms stronger,
rain drops bigger, and
hot spells hotter and longer.

Lush grasslands
are turning to deserts
where plants struggle to grow.
Forest fires, floods, and hurricanes
are happening more and more often.

All that extra heat in the air
is melting the glaciers and the ice sheets
at the North and South Poles.
As the ice melts,
waters rise and rivers overflow.
And because ice works like a mirror
and bounces heat back into space,
less ice means warmer oceans
and a warmer world.

If the world keeps on getting hotter,

it will be harder and harder

for people, animals, and plants to survive.

Cities will flood,

which means that millions of people

will need to find new places to live.

And it's not just humans that will be in trouble.

Many more plants and animals

may become extinct,

further upsetting Nature's harmony.

PART 4

TERRA CARTA

But wait!
We can bring Nature
back into balance.

Together we must imagine a brighter future
and work together across the world
to make it come true.

That means it's time for a Terra Carta,
a plan of action for the Earth.

It's time to agree . . .

WE WILL get energy from renewable sources
like direct sunlight, wind, and water.

WE WILL capture carbon from the air
and trap it deep underground or recycle it into clean fuel.

WE WILL bring

wild plants

and animals

back to where

they used to live.

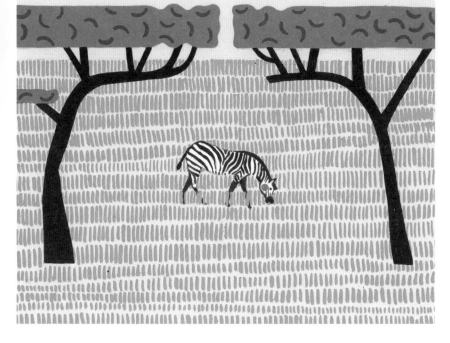

WE WILL make sure that
coral reefs,
forests,
savannas, and wetlands
grow and thrive.

WE WILL demand that everything we buy has a label that details its impact on Nature, People, and Planet.

That way, we can choose to buy products that help Nature, not hurt it.

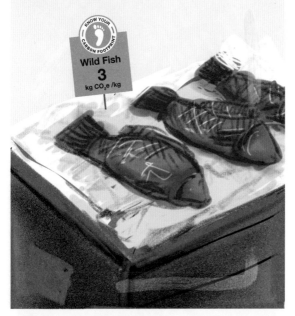

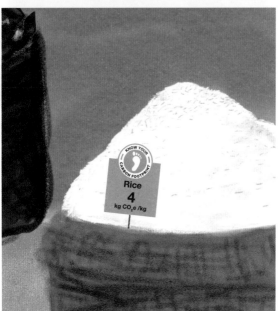

WE WILL listen to
the wisdom of people
whose ancestors
lived in harmony
with Nature for generations.

WE WILL work together
with artists, educators,
scientists, engineers,
farmers, designers,
and lots of other
smart thinkers
to find the best ways to keep
our planet,
and ourselves, healthy.

WE WILL demand that the leaders
of our countries and businesses
put Nature first.

WE WILL remind them
that if they don't act quickly,
all we depend on
may eventually collapse.

But if we work together,
Nature—including people—
will be around for
a very, very long time to come.

We CAN do this.

We MUST do this.

And we have to do it NOW.

Because . . .

IT'S
UP
TO US!

TERRA CARTA

For Nature, People & Planet

This book is based on the Terra Carta—a road map that was created by HRH The Prince of Wales and his Sustainable Markets Initiative to put Nature, People, and Planet at the heart of global value creation. This is the original language of the preface to the Terra Carta.

The supporters of the Terra Carta,

Commit to supporting and rapidly accelerating the world's transition towards a sustainable future.

Recognize the urgency of the global climate, biodiversity and health crises and the stewardship with which we must act.

Acknowledge that to build a sustainable future, the transition must focus on a robust, positive and parallel impact for Nature, People & Planet.

Recognize that ensuring the integrity of all ecosystems, on land and below water, requires that climate, oceans, desertification and biodiversity be treated as one common system and addressed simultaneously.

Acknowledge that we need to make health our goal; individual health, community health, economic health and the health of our Natural resources (e.g. soil, air and water).

Take into account the value of diversity, recognizing that diversity is a strength that gives resilience to communities, systems and organizations.

Recognize the importance of "local"—local traditions, languages and cultures along with local products, jobs and sustainability—and how these "locals" connect and support each other in the wider tapestry of regional and global systems.

Acknowledge that Nature underpins the inherent prosperity, well-being and future of all people and the one planet we share. Further, that the restoration of the Natural world is of common benefit to all humankind irrespective of borders.

Acknowledge that the required global trajectory is a sustainable one, where the private sector has a critical role to play. To accelerate along this trajectory, a "future of industry" and "future of economy" approach must be taken.

Take into account the need to ensure a skilled workforce and a cadre of leaders that are prepared to participate in a fair, inclusive, equitable and just transition towards a sustainable future.

Recognize that to scale sustainable solutions and investment, crossborder and longer-term "mega" projects need to be explored, underscoring the importance of public, private and philanthropic collaboration.

Acknowledge the need for net zero commitments to be achieved by 2050 and, where possible, much sooner. Setting more ambitious timelines will emphasize and catalyze immediate action while encouraging continuous innovation and improvement.

Undertake to collaborate, share knowledge and ideas to propel the world towards sustainability at a faster pace through public, private and philanthropic collaboration.

---

https://www.sustainable-markets.org/terra-carta/
Scan to find out more about the Terra Carta.

https://www.re-tv.org/
Scan to see videos of how to live in harmony with Nature.

Profiles of the Illustrators

The 33 illustrators who have contributed to this project come from around the globe.
Their styles vary widely, but here they come together to support children and to
express the urgency that we all join together to create a sustainable future.

Phùng Nguyên Quang & Huỳnh Kim Liên | VIETNAM | COVER, PAGES 46–47

Quang & Liên love illustrating animals and nature. They have collaborated on books published in a number of countries, often under the pen name KAA. Their illustrations are influenced by the folk culture of Vietnam and elsewhere in Asia.

Fotini Tikkou | GREECE | PAGES viii–1

Fotini is an illustrator and ceramic artist. She has an MA from Athens School of Fine Arts. She began her career as an illustrator in 2009 working mostly on children's books. Her work includes editorial illustrations, book covers, art licensing, pattern design, and ceramics.

Mehrdokht Amini | UK | PAGE 9

Mehrdokht Amini is an Iranian-British children's book illustrator living in London. She loves to study different cultures and communities to gain a better understanding and appreciation of all people.

Peter Sís | CZECH REPUBLIC / USA | ENDSHEETS

PHOTO BY JAN SLAVÍK

Peter was born in Brno. Today he lives and works as an artist, author, and filmmaker in New York City. He has created award-winning animations, tapestries, and murals and was recipient of the 2012 Hans Christian Andersen medal for illustration

Raúl Colón | USA | PAGES 2-3

Raúl is a prolific children's book illustrator with multiple honors to his credit, including two Pura Belpre awards. A proud New Yorker, he has also illustrated *New Yorker* covers and articles in the *New York Times* and even painted a mural in a New York subway station.

Sydney Smith | CANADA | PAGES 10–11

Sydney Smith is a picture book illustrator whose accolades include four successive *New York Times* Best Illustrated Children's Book of the Year citations and two Kate Greenaway medals. He lives in Halifax, Nova Scotia, with his wife and two sons.

Stuart Armstrong | USA | PAGES i, 1, 11, 21, 33, and 56

Stuart lives in Maryland, near Washington, DC. He grew up with 19th-century books filled with exquisite engravings, etchings, and woodcuts. The drama of black and white illustration always influenced the art he did for *National Geographic* and *The Washington Post*.

Murat Kalkavan | TURKEY | PAGES 4–5

Murat Kalkavan is an illustrator based in Istanbul. He enjoys creating funny and humorous character designs, and visuals for video games. He always tries to bring humor into his illustrations because he likes the positive effect it has on people.

Vanina Starkoff | ARGENTINA / BRAZIL | PAGES 12–13

Vanina Starkoff was born in Argentina and now lives in Brazil. The illustrator of more than 20 books, she has won awards in international competitions in Mexico, China, and Brazil. She loves living near the sea, among the birds and the trees.

Luisa Uribe | COLOMBIA | PAGES ii–iii

Luisa has illustrated many acclaimed picture books, including *Your Name is a Song* (Innovation Press), which was named one of *Time Magazine's* 10 Best Children Books of 2020. She lives surrounded by her ever-growing library.

Poonam Mistry | UK | PAGES 6–7

Poonam Mistry is a freelance illustrator of Indian heritage currently living in the UK. Her style incorporates her love of color, nature, folk art, and fables. Poonam describes her artwork as a celebration of patterns found all over the world.

Wesley Bedrosian | USA | PAGES 14–15

Wesley Bedrosian's work has appeared in *The New York Times* and *The Wall Street Journal*. He currently teaches and lectures at Massachusetts College of Art and Design in Boston. Wes lives in Massachusetts with his wife and two sons.

Gunnella | ICELAND | PAGES vi–vii

Gunnella is a painter, born and raised in Reykjavik. Old traditional houses, landscapes, people, and farming, painted in bright colors mixed with humor and joy, reflect her roots and heritage. The piece in this book reflects forestation initiatives in Iceland today.

Estelí Meza | MEXICO | PAGE 8

Estelí Meza was born in Mexico City. She studied Design and Visual Communication and has a Masters Degree in Visual Arts from the National Autonomous University of Mexico. She has published books in Mexico, Spain, the UAE, and the USA.

Nick Hayes | UK | PAGES 16–17

Nick Hayes is a writer and illustrator who lives on a boat on the River Thames. He is the creator of four graphic novels. His most recent book, *The Book of Trespass* is a *Sunday Times* Bestseller that tells the history of land ownership and how the public is often excluded from nature.

Rutu Modan | ISRAEL | PAGES 18–19

PHOTO BY HANAN ASSOR

Rutu Modan is an Israeli illustrator and comics artist. Her graphic novels and illustrated children's books have been translated into 15 languages and received international awards. She is a regular contributor to the *New Yorker* and the *New York Times Magazine*.

Sally Deng | USA | PAGES 30–31

Sally Deng creates drawings and paintings in her Los Angeles studio. Her award-winning illustrations have appeared in the *New York Times*, NPR, the *Atlantic* and more, as well as in her children's book, *Skyward*. She also exhibits art in galleries across the USA.

Musa Omusi | KENYA | PAGES 40–41

Musa Omusi is a prolific illustrator from Nairobi. His work is inspired by the world around him: the bright colors, vibrant patterns, and bold shapes. He works with other artists that he meets along his way to bring peace, love, and joy to the world.

Gwen Keraval | FRANCE | PAGES 20–21

Gwen Keraval graduated from Emile Cohl Art School in Lyon. He likes to work with geometric shapes and symmetrical layouts, using reduced color palettes in vintage tones, in order to bring a special mood to all kinds of subjects, from editorial to magazine and publishing.

Owen Davey | UK | PAGES 32–33

Owen Davey is the lead illustrator on the multi-award-winning app *Two Dots* and has produced many award-winning picture books, which have been published all over the world. His title *Fanatical About Frogs* was shortlisted for the Blue Peter Book Awards 2020.

Leah Marie Dorion | CANADA | PAGES 42–43

Leah is a Métis teacher, artist, illustrator, and writer currently living near Prince Albert, Saskatchewan. Her artwork celebrates the strength and resilience of indigenous women and families. Leah believes that women are the first teachers to the next generation.

Isol | ARGENTINA | PAGES 22–23

PHOTO BY VAGELIS ZAVOS

Isol is an Argentinian illustrator and author of 26 books in 17 languages. She won the Astrid Lindgren Memorial Award, a Golden Apple, the Prix Jeunesse, was shortlisted for an Emmy Award, and has twice been a finalist for the Hans Christian Andersen award.

Su Jung Jang | UK/SOUTH KOREA | PAGES 34–35

Su Jung Jang is an illustrator, visual artist, and lecturer based in Seoul and London. She creates delicate and subtle images by collaging her drawings with other media. Su Jung enjoys exploring the relationship between humans and nature in her artwork.

Sally Caulwell | IRELAND | PAGES 44–45

Sally Caulwell is a Dublin-based illustrator and designer. Sally's style pairs a gentle aesthetic with clean graphic lines. Playing with geometry, she likes to distill things down to simple forms. Her work features balanced compositions which use repetition, pattern, and color.

Nick Sharratt | UK | PAGES 24–25

Nick Sharratt has illustrated over 300 children's books. He's worked with the most popular children's authors in the UK, and he also illustrates his own award-winning titles. His picture books *Shark in the Park* and *You Choose* have been adapted for the stage.

Paolo Domeniconi | ITALY | PAGES 36–37

Paolo Domeniconi began working in children's books illustrating a series of classic fairy tales. He has now illustrated more than 50 books and collaborated with publishers around the world. His artworks are published in Italy, Spain, UK, USA, Korea, China, and Taiwan.

Harmony Becker | USA | PAGES 48–49

Harmony Becker is a graphic novel author and illustrator. She illustrated George Takei's Eisner Award winning graphic novel *They Called Us Enemy* and wrote and illustrated the graphic novel *Himawari House*. She loves being a person living on the Earth.

Blak Douglas | AUSTRALIA | PAGES 26–27

Blak Douglas was born in Western Sydney. His father is Aboriginal and his mother is Australian. He is trained in illustration, photography, and graphic design. Observing a family of artisans, he is a self-trained painter influenced by environmental and political issues.

Victoria Fomina | RUSSIA | PAGE 38

Victoria Fomina graduated from Moscow State Academy of Architecture. Her interests include painting, graphics, design, and illustration. She has illustrated over 50 books. Victoria has received numerous prizes in illustration competitions around the world.

Barry Falls | UK | PAGE 54

Barry Falls grew up in rural Northern Ireland, where he spent a lot of time drawing pictures and writing stories to go with them. At art college in Belfast, he was very excited to learn that he could do this for a living! He has won multiple awards for illustration.

Ye Luying | CHINA | PAGES 28–29

Ye Luying is an illustrator and lecturer at the China Academy of Art. She is fascinated by the beauty of Asian culture and includes unique interpretations of it in her work. Her many picture books, such as *Goddess of the Luo River* and *Mulan,* have won numerous awards.

Reza Dalvand | IRAN | PAGE 39

Reza Dalvand is an illustrator and author of children's books. His art focuses on early childhood developmental psychology. In his books, Reza brings to life realistic and imaginary worlds, immersing his audience in a colorful and magical environment.

Kumiko Horibe | JAPAN | BACK COVER

Kumiko lives in Tokyo and graduated from Joshibi College of Art and Design and MJ Illustration School. Her work was selected for the Bologna Children's Book Exhibition in 2021. She tries to make the hearts of those who see her work kind and happy.

THE PRINCE'S FOUNDATION

It's Up to Us and the story it tells come at a very important moment for Nature, People, and Planet. Our climate is changing, our forests and animal habitats are under threat, and our oceans are being polluted. Time is quickly running out to protect our planet's precious well-being—but, as this wonderful book shows us, it's not too late!

At The Prince's Foundation, we strive to find the best possible ways to help bring Nature, People, and Planet back into balance. As part of our mission, we use our headquarters at Dumfries House, in Scotland, UK, to showcase examples of how to restore and maintain Nature in balance across a wide range of interests from health and well-being, education, and horticulture to art, architecture, farming, craft, and cooking.

The work of The Prince's Foundation is inspired by HRH The Prince of Wales's ideas about Harmony. This is a way of understanding that everything in Nature is connected. Everything we do should be understood as being part of the fabric of Nature. That means appreciating that the actions we take have an impact on the rest of the world, not just on ourselves or on our species. Harmony is about acting in ways that put the well-being of people and planet first. It proposes that only by working together can we bring Nature back into balance and only in that way can the Harmony of Nature be restored. It is this belief that makes it our great pleasure to be a partner in the creation of this beautiful book *It's Up to Us*.

We hope this simple but powerful nonfiction book, and the remarkable illustrations within it, will inspire people of all ages to learn about and engage with the enormous challenges our planet faces as well as the positive actions we can all take to help protect it. If you would like to learn more about the many themes touched on in this book, our educational team at The Prince's Foundation has created a wide range of extra activities and learning resources that can be found by following the link or scanning the QR code below.

It's up to us!

Simon Sadinsky
Executive Director (Education)

DUMFRIES HOUSE

Cumnock KA18 2NJ, 19–22 Charlotte Road, London EC2A 3SG | enquiries@princes-foundation.org

https://princes-foundation.org/education/its-up-to-us

Glossary-Index

Carbon Footprint

The carbon footprint of the electricity used to print this book (see back cover) was calculated using measurements carried out by the printer, Santiago Offset, and the Mexican National Electric System's 2020 emissions factor, published by the Mexican Center for Energy Control (CENACE). The other carbon footprint data included in the book and on the back cover come from the following sources:

"How much carbon dioxide is produced per kilowatt hour of U.S. electricity generation?" U.S. Energy Information Administration, December 15, 2020. https://www.eia.gov/tools/faqs/faq.php?id=74&t=11

Richie, Hannah. "You want to reduce the carbon footprint of your food? Focus on what you eat, not whether your food is local." Our World in Data, 24 Jan. 2020, University of Oxford, https:// ourworldindata.org/food-choice-vs-eating-local

"Trees help tackle climate change." European Environment Agency, January 6, 2012. https://www.eea.europa.eu/articles/forests-health-and-climate-change/key-facts/trees-help-tackle-climate-change

About the Fibonacci spiral

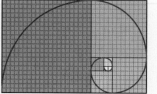

The Fibonacci spiral is a pattern that occurs throughout Nature. In this book, you can see it highlighted in a vine, a chameleon, a human thumbprint, a hurricane, and a flower. The amazing thing about this spiral is that it follows a mathematical pattern known as the Fibonacci sequence. That sequence starts with 0 and 1 and continues by adding the last two numbers in a row together to get the next number, like this: 0, 1, 1, 2, 3, 5, 8, 13, 21 and so on. You can see the way the spiral relates to the sequence by drawing a series of squares with sides that follow the sequence. Start with two 1 x 1 squares and put a 2 x 2 square next to them. Then add a 3 x 3 square next to the 1 x 1 and the 2 x 2 squares. Keep going as long as you want. Then draw a spiral that curves through the squares from corner to corner in a smooth spiral.

We hope you enjoy this book for many years to come, but when you are finished with it please help to prolong its life and help the planet by gifting it or donating it so that others may enjoy it, too.